THE POWER
TO PRESS-ON

"I wrote this book for those with a burning desire to achieve their wildest dreams."

- **Edmond EddiNations**
(Performance Coach, Author & Entrepreneur)

"Using Conversational stories of some of the world's greatest achievers, and their personal stories on the journey to success, Edmond EddiNations has highlighted powerful nuggets for achieving the impossible and reaching to the sky heights."

- **Lucky Lebepe**
(Author and Founder of TLC & Seboka Consultants)

"For those that want to be entertained, while reaching their life batteries."

- **Howard Zondo**
(Author of Young, Black & Powerful, and Lessons from a Domestic Worker)

THE POWER
TO PRESS-ON

The power used by every achiever to
succeed at their wildest dreams

EDMOND EDDINATIONS

ISBN 978-0-620-86422-0 (print)

ISBN 978-0-620-86423-7 (e-book)

All designs of the book including cover and the layout were proudly designed by Minas Media Group.

Published in South Africa

By Minas Media Group

In Partnership with EddiNations Int.

To

Thembisile Masemola, Khutso Shokoane, and Madira Mahlase,

Thank you for your sacrificial support in my dreams and for ensuring that this book gets published. I could've not done it without you.

For

This book is for everyone burning with a wish to achieve their wildest dreams

Contents

Foreword x

Introduction xii

Chapter 01 **POWERS OF CHANGE** 17

   1. Physical Power **18**
      Laws of Positional Power 19
      A Force Working Against Us 21
      It Takes a Force 22
   2. Functional Power **23**
      The Human Mind 24
      Mentally Programmed 26
   3. Intellectual Power **27**
      When Things Fall Apart 28
      All Segments Combined 30
      Big Trouble in Labor Force 31
      Just for Starters 32

Chapter 02 **MISUNDERSTANDING OF PASSION** 35

   What is Passion? **36**
      Look at Love 37
      It's not a Feeling 39
      Like any other Energy 40
      Passionate but. 42
      More than Passion 43

Chapter 03 **FORCES AGAINST SUCCESS** 46

Law of gravity **48**

Every time you go up 49

Law of Arrow dynamics 51

Chapter 04 **THE POWER OF HUMAN BEINGS** **54**

Our Source of Creativity 56

Like God 58

After our own Image & Likeness 60

More than a Miracle 61

It's in you! 64

Chapter 05 **THE POWER TO PRESS-ON** **67**

Purpose **68**

Vision **70**

Life wasters 71

Typical Israelites 72

Sense of Achieving **74**

Steve Job's Secret Power 76

From Valleys to Cyber 77

Mental System 78

Chapter 06 **FIVE TRAITS OF PEOPLE WITH PURPOSE** **83**

1. **They're Positive** **85**

   Story of Watson (IBM) 86

   Thomas & Steve 87

   It takes Purpose 88

2. **They Plan** **90**

   Not a Goose 92

   Phobia of Planning 93

   Misconception of plan B **94**

3. **They Prepare** **97**

   Value of Preparation 99

I was being prepared 100

Steve and his Macintosh 103

4. They Pick Well **104**

Divorcing the Richest Man 105

Winnie Madikizela-Mandela 107

My Friend's Story 109

5. They Take Risk **110**

It takes Risk 111

Gambling saves FedEx 112

The Price Tag 113

Package **115**

Chapter 07 **DEVELOPING A PURPOSE DRIVEN LIFE** **119**

It Takes Process 120

Find Yourself 121

Interests **122**

Weaknesses vs Strengths **124**

Role of Weaknesses 125

Redirection 126

My Fair Share 128

Your Future **130**

Focus on your Strengths 131

Practical Steps **133**

Reading Tip:

When you feel disconnecting from what you're reading, please take a break. Rest your mind for an hour, then continue later.

I do it all the time!

Don't read to finish, read to learn and enjoy!

Foreword

PROPHET LUCKY LEBEPE

*L*ife can be hard, unfair, and at times cruel. We all need the energizing fuel that refreshes us to get up, shake off the dust and ashes of defeat, and keep running towards the finishing line. After all, great success doesn't lie in great starts, but excellent finishings.

The Power to press-on is an essential tool for performance enhancement. After I read through this book, I could only picture an athlete in a marathon catching a flying bottle of water from his trainer to cool himself off with a swift sip and pour some of it on his hot, weary body to keep pressing to the mark. Life is a race, and just like athletics, not all who chase their dreams will eventually enjoy their achievements and realization. Some will quit out of exhaustion and others out of emergency casualties.

We all need support mechanisms to boast our confidence during hard trials of our pursuit of success. I'm happy to come across this documented boaster that will resuscitate lost passions for those who throw in the towel while kindling those in the racecourse for success with the eternal flame of courage, and who never dare to give up.

Using conversational stories of some of the world's most famous achievers, and their personal stories on the journey to success, Edmond EddiNations has highlighted powerful nuggets for achieving the impossible and reaching to sky heights.

I recommend this book to those who wish to leave no stone unturned, change their worlds, and who dare to succeed against all the odds. Every dreamer and every chaser of higher goals must own a copy of this book

Introduction

for you to achieve any goal, whether a business goal, building the most significant inventory, losing weight, gaining muscles, winning idols, releasing a single track, acting on television, being a movie star, running 50 km Marathon, being the best footballer or even the best golfer, the ability to press-on will be required.

Like John C Maxwell says, *"There is nothing easy worth following in life. Everything you want is up-hilled."* And for you to go and get it, you'll have to be prepared to press on the hills. Tenacious energy is required to reach your destiny. And the ability to press-on is what distinguishes achievers from losers. When I talk about losers, I am not referring to those who meet failure, but rather those who decide to abort purpose by giving up. Those who choose to give up permanently can, therefore, be as losers. While achievers have learned the art of pressing on, losers have similarly learned the art of giving up.

Without being harsh on the dropouts, let me grant them a bit of justice. I've learned that people who ultimately quit, don't stop because they are lazy, or because they don't want it as bad as their next breath. Being quick to throw such stickers is an injustice. Some people strived hard on the idea they've quit. Some were immersively obsessed with the idea they've promptly forsaken. At some point they pushed, but not for long. Some pressed for months until they couldn't anymore. Others urged a few years until they couldn't anymore. Not because they got lazy, not because they didn't want it as bad as their next breath, but because they didn't have the power to press-on.

Everything eventually runs out of power; human beings are no anomaly. Cars flow out of petrol, cellphones drop out of battery, tractors flow out of diesel, some stoves and refrigerators flow out of gas, and even the power station supplying us with electricity needs constant refiling of coals to keep generating power. So even human beings ultimately reach power outflow, the ability to keep dreaming, the energy to stay positive, and the vigor to keep pressing towards their goals.

If electricity is there to recharge our cellphones, petrol stations are there to refill our car tanks, and coal mines being there to refill the power stations, then what is there to refill human's power to keep pressing on? Unawareness of the need to be refilled has led many to think it's the end of the journey at a state of low battery. Those who packed their bags and threw in the towel, did it because they assumed a state of the low battery as a dead battery not knowing that there is power made available to renew their hopes, energy, dreams, and journeys.

For you to persist weighting towards your dreams, there is dynamism you need. Without power, nothing changes, and without strength, nothing moves. For your car to convey you to work, there has to be a power to run. For your cellphone to make calls, there has to be a power to function. Even for you to make a financial move to the next level, there has to be an intellectual power.

This book will introduce you to the power you need to achieve your wildest aspirations. It took this power for all successful people you admire to be where they are. For you to put in the bag the next goal, you'll need to engage this power. The last chapter will give you practical steps on how to discover this power, as well as how to utilize it. This book wasn't composed to motivate you, but to practically empower you. Please take it as a gym, every chapter being the equipment you need to develop your future into an artistic shape of success.

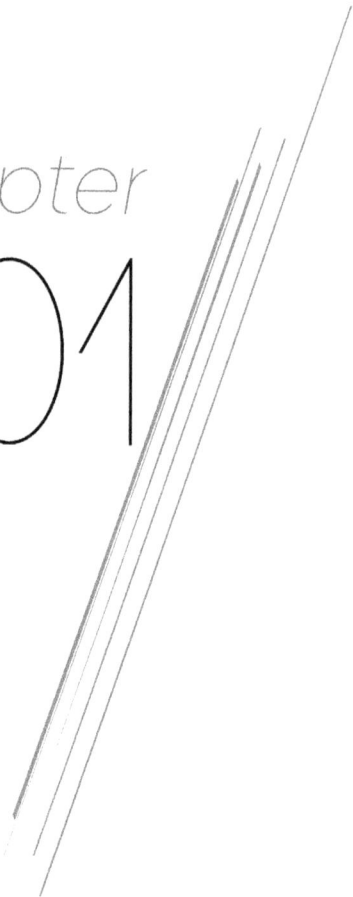

Chapter

01

POWERS
OF CHANGE

1 Physical Power

The most common way people give up their power is by thinking they don't have any.

— Alice Walker

$\mathcal{P}$ ositional power is a force required to move physically from point A to B. In science, potential energy it's a mass of a stationary object against gravity, and kinetic energy includes velocity. They only teach these staff in objects, and we never thought about them working in our lives. Yet these are quite potent staff when considered in our lives.

For example, when I look at these forces, I begin to apprehend having to sit with potential being obscure. It's arduous to stay viable with unproductive potential than it is when it is applied. Kinetic energy is potential energy on the go. When potential leap by faith, it transforms into kinetic. You'll realize when you calculate kinetic energy that the higher the speed, means the mass is lightweight. The lightweight travel faster than a heavyweight

Laws of Positional Power

Perhaps all you aspire in life is to graduate with a Ph.D. and sharpen your career afterward. That is not an influential dream to the world, except in your life and family, but contrasted to the world's needs, its manor. Hence, you'll need to move at a higher speed, achieve it as early as possible. I know many young people under the age of 30 who already obtained such milestones. How come? It's a lightweight dream. Even possessing millions of rands in your account is a thin dream. You can rob a bank and have those millions. You can sell the farm of your father and have those millions. If your goal is to be a millionaire, then you can achieve that at a younger age, because it's lightweight. If it's more for you than it is for the world, then it's lightweight.

Secondly, the more substantial the idea, the slower the pace. How long did it take Steve Job to build the giant Apple Company? How long did it take Dubai to develop its most architectural buildings that attract tourists all over the world? How long did it take Nelson Mandela and his struggle fighters to overturn the apartheid system in South

Africa? Maybe things seem to be overdue in your life, not because you're not yielding your best, but because you're carrying a more substantial dream.

The predicament begins when a person carrying a more substantial dream starts to compare themselves with someone with a minuscule goal. It's easy to be intimidated in your idea of improving the world when you see someone already a millionaire or with a Ph.D. before age 25 while being 30, still broke, and striving to get your idea off the ground. This inclination begins when you don't concede the law of kinetic energy, that the lighter the weight, the faster the speed and the more substantial the weight, the slower the pace.

The problem of potential energy is that while the object remains still, there's always a force pulling it down. Gravity doesn't care whether you're moving or stuck, it insistently pulls you down.

A Force Working Against Us

Depending on your beliefs, you'll link gravity to a lot of restraints in life. Spiritual people consider evil as gravity, while the non-spiritual people regard it as life issues. I also believe evil is working around the clock to tear us down, emotionally, physically, and even intellectually. While we call it life when we transpire the most, the devil remains the force behind all negativity happenings in the world. *Make use of every opportunity, for these days are full of evil,* is the bible's bits of advice.

The other day I assured one lady that whether she induce or not, she's demure or not, she's afraid of approaching people or not, whether she doesn't like disturbing people or not. Whether she's pursuing her dreams or not, life will not commiserate on her. Attacks will come even when you're not striking, you'll be hurt even when you're innocent, and you can't expect life to be lenient on you because you're a good person. Even Jesus, the man without any sin, was crucified and executed naked on the cross. At least we're not about to be crucified, but we'll have our fair share.

The reason I was sharing this with her is that I wanted to show her that it's better to bother people pursuing your dreams than to sit back and still suffer. It's more salutary to be on your feet fighting for a better life than to hold back and still grieve. A person who suffers trying to achieve their dreams is way better than the one who suffers doing nothing.

Sadly, with the potential of being the next great thing, many are still pushed against the walls. And the longer you sit with your potential; the more gravity will pull you down

It Takes a Force

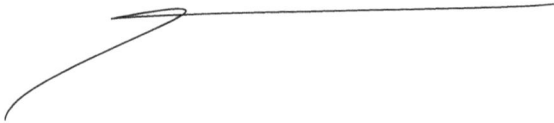

But to move physically from position A to B, you need physical energy. It takes a force to drive your car, to fly a plane, to sail the ship, and sprint in sports. Without power, you can't move. Everyone must compel to reconstruct their potential energy into kinetic energy, the energy that produces effects, the energy that makes things happen, and awake dogs out of their kennels to bark over the fence.

Every overweight person carries the potential of a slimmer body, a miniature person has the potential of masculinity, and an unhealthy person has the potential of health. But for these people to change their physical conditions, they'll need to apply physical power to themselves. To move from the body of overweight to a slimmer, physical energy is required. You'll require physical strength to transcend from tiny to a muscular body, and the same thing goes to advancing your health. The reason why these people will never change, apart from preferences, is that they're not willing to apply physical energy.

2 Functional Power

Minds are like parachutes - they only function when opened
— *Thomas Dewar*

$\mathcal{F}$unctional power is the dynamism acting within operational objects. It is the vigor responsible for the positional control. While the positional power is in velocity *(inactions)*, this one is in watts *(in producing)*. It provides movements, and without it, there can never be an impetus. For the car to move, the engine has to produce energy. For the power station to share electricity, the generators have to produce energy. For mining shafts to provide gold, the generators have to give power, and even for humans to move; the body has to offer energy.

This power works in everything that's functioning. Also, our cellphones and laptops need functioning power to respond to our demands. The lights in the house, the stoves, and refrigerators, everything depends on the functional ability to fulfill desires.

The Human Mind

The brain is the central system of functional power. It is our brain that creates energy for us to function, not the heart. The heart pumps blood throughout the body via the circulatory system, supplying oxygen and nutrients to the tissues and removing carbon dioxide and other wastes. We know that from the medical experience, someone declared brain damaged can no longer function, but to only repose on a bed in life-supporting machines. Although the person's heart still bumps adequately, due to the damage in their brain, they cease to function.

The brain is the most powerful organ in your body. It can keep the body at function, even in disabilities. Dysfunctional ears don't stop deaf people from information, and dysfunctional eyes don't stop the blind from moving. Therefore, Poverty shouldn't stop you from dreaming, debts shouldn't stop you from planning, and even lack of support shouldn't prompt you to abort your goals. With an active brain, you still bear the ability to function.

Many people are inadequate in breaking the circle of poverty, not because their circumstances are too oppressive to break, but because they've put to demise the component of better functionality. Laziness of the mind is worse than laborious idleness. Someone lazy to work but diligent in his thinking can find a way to get his ideas done, but if you're lazy to think, there is no hope for you, except to be subjected into slavery of someone else's dreams.

If you look into all successful people in the world held in high reverence, they breed from less privileged backgrounds. Steve Job's parents gave him up for adoption. Oprah Winfrey was born in a low-income family and suffered sexual abuse as a kid. David, in the bible, grew up despised by his own family. Starbucks founder Howard Schultz grew up in a housing complex for the poor. During an interview with the Mirror, he said, *"Growing up, I always felt like I was on the other side of the tracks. I knew the people on the other side had more resources, more money, happier family. And for some reason, I don't know why or how I wanted to climb over that fence and achieve something beyond what people were saying was possible."*

Without the power to function, you only exist, and to start living, you need to start thinking. *To start living, you must start thinking.* The day you stop thinking, it is the day you stop living

Mentally Programmed

I've come to realize that the reason many people fail to function better mentally is that their minds where programmed to fail. From childhood, we've been fed fear, negativity and comfort. We're afraid of pursuing our ideas because we were narrated as inadequate for better things in life. We don't believe we can because that's how we were raised to believe. Our minds were programmed to function for failure. Too many vermins were embedded in our mental systems, and now we remain bolted.

To see a change in your life, you'll have to reprogram your thinking. Flash out all the vermins in your mind, and then embed new profitable mindsets and beliefs. Neuroscientists report that most beliefs governing our lives were programmed in our subconscious minds the first seven years of our childhood. Because our conscious mind was in a state of hypnosis, we received whatever we were told or observed without second questioning. Sadly, many of us were negatively programmed to fearful and failing lives. To change our lives then, we must change programs in our minds, and we can only do that by repetition, invariably affirming yourself into what you want to become.

3 Intellectual Power

Intelligence is the effort to do the best you can at your particular job: the quality that gives dignity to that job. whether it happens to be scrubbing a floor or running a corporation.

— James C. Penney

The Intellectual power helps you advance in positions within an organization and to higher financial class in life. For this power to effectively deliver better outcomes in any endeavor, three elements must all come to play, knowledge, understanding, and wisdom. These elements are essential to the performance of intellectual power when they're all in use. *"With wisdom, a house is built, with understanding, it is established (or it stands), and with knowledge, its rooms are filled with treasures."* The biblical perspective of intellectual power.

For you to merit a promotion at work, increase the profit margin of your business, become an influential figure in your community, you'll have to activate three virtues of intellectual power. If you strive without some of these virtues, you'll not perform to your best abilities. According to the biblical perspective, you might find yourself having treasures without a house to store them, or building things that can't supersede the test of time.

When Things Fall Apart

A lot of businesses close down as a failure to well articulate customer's needs. It took intellectual power for Henry Ford to know his consumers' needs even before they could realize. At the invention of Ford, he said, *"If I asked my customers what they wanted, they would have said a faster horse."* He was able to give them something much better than a faster horse. But not every investor is as intelligent as Ford. Apple swiped away Blackberry's market with an on-screen keyboard. When Nokia hesitated to embrace the system of android from Google, Samsung quickly jumped in and overshadowed them.

Lack of understanding in relationships has induced a lot of marriages to fall apart. After living together for 15 years, you'll still hear one partner saying, *"He doesn't get me."* The root cause of many divorces is the absence of understanding of the partner's behavior, language, passions, interests, desires, and needs. And we know from the bible that without understanding, a house shall not stand.

Without wisdom, legacies eventually break down and career shutters. Many people can't finish projects, they can't finally tie the knot, they can't buy their own houses, and their common excuse is very classic, *"Lack of money."* I would agree with that if I didn't meet financially underprivileged people who managed to marry, build houses, and build businesses from nothing. The truth is that the lack of wisdom is the reason people can't sustain nor accomplish goals with fewer resources.

All Segments Combined

To be merely informed it's not enough. You'll also need to possess understanding and wisdom to know how to be productive with your knowledge. When all the three segments of intellectual power begin to work together in your life, your career progresses, your business expands, and your talent becomes profitable. You'll start to break out of debts, out of financial crisis into good streams of financial in-flow.

To increase your intellectual power, you need to increase your knowledge, understanding, and wisdom. That's why the higher the position advertised, the higher the knowledge and skills required. Skills reflect how well you understand that subject, and how wisely you've functioned in it. As human beings, we've always been advancing through intellectual and functional powers. And to keep winning even at this age of technological slenderness of robotics and artificial intelligence, we'll need more of these powers engaged in our lives. Those who still rely on physical ability to earn bread will be supplanted by machines that can perform tasks much faster with exponential results.

Big Trouble in Labor Force

We've seen various private companies retrenching workers, cutting business expenditures by closing some of their branches, in a quest for digital migration. Standard Bank closed 100 branches in 2019, McDonald introduced on-screen ordering systems, and Pick n' Pay also introduced a self-service teller. We've also seen Alibaba showcasing a robot that can do the waiter's duties while the other takes care of stock packing. Many machinery inventions will continue to be deployed into the workplace, particularly within the private sector, to replace human labor. And industries such as textile, manufacturing, mining, retail, construction, and perhaps even in agriculture will be more affected by the 4th industrial revolution because they employ the majority of human labor.

It's very crucial for anyone who desires greener pastures in these times to utilize the functional and intellectual powers. You'll have to be innovative enough to solve problems, creative enough to make your solutions work, and a critical thinker who's able to see possibilities out of compressed situations. The only way to advance against robotics is to do what they can't do, which is to think. However, being a critical thinker or a highly qualified person is still not enough to fulfill your ideas. You can be the most significant thinker, the most intellectual person, and even the most physically fit but still not achieve your goals. Many people are stuck with great ideas that can propel their lives into glorious destinies because they cannot press-on.

Just for Starters

All these powers we've talked about isn't enough to help you achieve your goals. They're essential to start the journey, but not adequate to finish the game. You can plot great plans with your wisdom, have a great understanding of what it takes to win, knowledge to implement great strategy, physical muscles, and fitness to deploy into the game, but if the team lacks the power to press on, they can make your game plan a failure.

How many wise rated people have you met living a life of defeat? How many highly intelligent people who used to outshine the entire class who've remained average in life? How many health attractive freaks who eventually suffer strokes and heart attacks? Indeed, the life race is not for the fast runners, nor victories for the masculinity, neither high earnings for those with degrees. With all our degrees, beauty, wisdom, fitness, passions in pursuit of our dreams, we'll all face an option to either press on or plateau. Someone without a degree, portraying the tenacious spirit of pressing on, will surpass the one who possesses a degree without the ability to press on. At the end of all our qualifications, success comes down to this one common trait: the ability to press on.

A degree won't keep you going when all doors are banged on your face, and an idea won't advance you when nobody is willing to listen. The truth we were never told is that these things are meant to be foundations, not the whole recipe of success. Today many people feel betrayed because after solely depending on these for success, they encounter unexpected disappointments.

If it only required an idea to succeed, then everyone would be a high achiever. Let's face it, even that burger by the roadside was once fascinated about a particular concept. And if only degrees were required to succeed, people like Richard Branson would've never had a chance to succeed. But after dropping out of grade 6, Richard went on to build a billion-dollar business at Virgin Group. The man didn't even make an effort to at least graduate from the primary level, yet today most qualified people fly first class in his airlines. The likes of Richard Branson, Bill Gates, Steve Jobs, Nelson Mandela, Warren Buffet, Patrice Motsepe, Richard Maponya, Jack Ma, and Elon Musk achieved their wildest dreams through the power of pressing on

Chapter

02

MISUNDER-STANDING OF PASSION

What is Passion?

"Passion is energy. Feel the power that comes from focusing on what excites you."

— *Oprah Winfrey*

A lot of people will tell you that it takes a passion to succeed. In one of his interviews, Steve Job says these words, *"It's really hard to succeed, and if you're not passionate about the thing you do, you'll give up. Because it's hard, you have to love what you do."* While I concur with Steve and many other speakers who advocate for passion, I sense a missing link when it comes to the topic of passion. I don't think we've taken enough time to dive deeper into understanding its concept. Some people link it with love, like in this case of Steve, and others connect it with desire and motivation, while others can link it with inspiration. In other words, from what we hear from people, we can presume that passion is love, desire, motivation, and inspiration. Well, we have others who take it step further, like Brandon Buchard, who says, *"Don't be passionate; be obsessed."* Brandon debates the fact that obsessing about what you do is more powerful than just being passionate. I agree with Brandon that it takes more than a passion for achieving.

Passion is energy, and like any other energy, it runs out. You'll not always feel passionate about your goals. So the question is: if it takes passion for pursuing my goal, and for the whole month, I don't feel excited about it, what do I do? Do I hang around the buildings and wait for passion to kick in again so I can continue the journey? Should I perform some exercises that will trigger my love back on?

If passion is love, desire, and motivation for our dreams, then like all of those things, we'll not always feel it. If two married people stay in the marriage as long as they feel the love for their spouses, then a lot of marriages are in trouble already. But this has to do with understanding the concept of love and passion more than the subject itself. Passion works if you know how it works.

Look at Love

Our biggest mistake is the assumption that love is a feeling. When people talk about love, they mostly speak from the perspective of their feelings. That's why we hear a lot of people saying, *"I was so in love with her... I loved you so much... There was a time when I used to love you."* Now, if you're a Christian, you'll realize that these statements are a contradiction to what the Bible teaches about love. To summarize the concept of love, the Bible shortly puts it this way, *"Love never ends."* Simple! Now, if love is a feeling, and love never ends, then how come people link love with past tense? Why do we tend to sound like love has ended? Does it?

We also carry the assumption that the evidence of love is the ability to get along. The day we can't withstand each other, we perceive it as a sign of dead love. Eventually, time proves this wrong when after a few years of separation, a couple that couldn't stand each other, blasted each other to the grave, and dragged each other through the mud. After years of finally living apart, getting the privilege of fresh air, beginning to regain weight and skin glow, finally meet each other and talk about, *"Let's try again."* How can two people who presumed their love finished even beyond repair, suddenly seem enthusiastic to cultivate the spark again?

Could this be because you can refill love? Or that it never dies? Or is it that certain things tend to overshadow love? But the ability to get along does not serve as a shred of evidence for love. You can get along even when you don't love each other, and you can love each other yet still grapple to get along. It doesn't take love to stay together, it takes understanding and embracing each other's personalities, strengths, and weaknesses. I mean, even enemies can get along because of a common enemy.

It's not a Feeling

Love is not a feeling, just like the wind is not the coldness. Just because it's windy, doesn't mean it will be cold, and just because it's cold, it doesn't mean there is wind. So just because I feel the breeze running through my arms, goosebumps in my stomach, and unstoppable swing of a smile on my face, with my blood flowing twice the standard rate all over my body, doesn't mean it's a sign of love. Love is not a feeling. Love is a conscious decision and an unconditional commitment to that decision. If you want to love someone, you study their character, strengths, weaknesses, and you see if you can live with all of those things then decide to love that person. After your observations, you unconditionally commit to loving that person. That is love, and because of its unconditional commitment, it won't end.

Not that I am planning to turn this book into love and romance, but I've shared the concept of love to demonstrate the similar misunderstanding we have about passion.

Like any other Energy

Passion is a desire. That's it! An excitement that serves as persuading energy to strive to achieve your dream. Like any other energy, whether it be energy to run, energy to brighten the house, energy to drive the car, and any different energy, passion also runs out. And like any energy, it can be renewed.

You'll not always feel passionate about your idea, and that doesn't mean you're not intense enough or don't love your idea enough. It just means the energy of your desire needs to be refilled.

When a couple that used to be so affectionate towards each other suddenly reach a point of *"less affection,"* they think love has died. Like the scenario I gave, being distant from each other for few years was a moment of refilling the affection, and they had no idea. That's why after those years, when affection gets refreshed, and then they meet again, they're engaging with the same energy as when they first met. So the same energy comes with the same thoughts they had before, the ideas that we can make it work and that we can be the happiest couple. They instantly want to try again. If they knew this from day one, they would've never gone through a messy separation. They could've taken proper steps to refill their passion for each other.

There'll come a period in your life, some of you you're already there, where you won't sense the passion in your dream, as troubles and disappointments of this life drained any spark of love in you. When that moment comes, it doesn't mean the goal isn't for you, and it doesn't mean it's the end of the road for you. It merely means that you're drained, and you need to recharge.

If we're going to keep telling people that it takes passion for succeeding and that the reason they give up is that they're not passionate enough, then we're better off without that mic and the pen in our hands. Our silent, in this case, will be much helpful than the words we speak and write.

Passionate but...

I know many people who are passionate about their talents, yet gave up and settled for lower living standards. I know people who sing their way to the store, with sweet voices that can strive on the Spotify charts with that of Ed Sheeran, but somehow don't believe they're adequate. Even on Sundays, I witness too many talented young people fearlessly expressing their talents, yet outside the church, they've given up on life, working in the wrong careers to survive. We surely can't say these people don't love what they do.

These people love what they do; passion is paraded all over their performances, and they want to shine forth, but they're stuck and have settled. Some things are very good at draining passion out of a person. Everyone with passion will face those things, and that's when the power to press on will be required for you to overcome. Fear, rejection, negative thoughts, critics, multiple failures and loses, and also disappointments, are some of the passion drainers we'll all encounter in pursuit of our dreams. Experience these things on a streak, and watch your passion running out of spark.

More than Passion

When these things hit you hard, your passion will need a rescue for you to be re-energized to keep striving for your dreams. Only the power to press on can rescue your love at this stage. So more than passion, you'll necessitate the ability to press on, more than a desire, you'll need the power to press on, and even more than love, you'll need the strength to press on. Because the ability to press on will make all these things work even at their localities of breaking, it will hold them together when they're falling apart. When a couple leans on the power to press on, dry affection will not make them fall apart. They'll be able to overcome the absence of affection, and they will be able to fix any predicament that arises because that power empowers you until your dream becomes a reality.

There is a variation between loving what you do and making what you love work. These two are not equivalent. Passion will make you like what you do. It will kindle a desire of love in you for your dream. But it won't get the job done; it won't make what you love work. Benny McCarthy loved what he did; he loved playing soccer. He was the best South African striker who went on to represent us in the biggest soccer league in the world,

English Premier League. But when Benny's career appeared to end in England, it showed that although it took a passion for getting him started, it didn't take a passion for making him a success, nor did it take love to sustain his career. While he was shining on top, Benny began to gain weight, and with Coaches becoming unimpressed, it killed his playing time. That was the end beginning of Benny's international career.

It took Benny the power to press on for him to have a great international career, pressing on to stay fit, pressing on to sharpen his skills, pressing on to stay ahead of the game, and when he began to lose the sight of that power, his career began to slow down to the end. It takes strength to press on for you to make what you love work.

Chapter

03

FORCES AGAINST SUCCESS

*W*hy is it so hard to make our dreams a reality, and why should we have to sweat to produce results? Why do we fail along the way, and why is success so hard to achieve? If you've never supplicated from life or God these questions, then it implies two things; your parents are wealthy or you still a minor teen.

Like gravity, there's a force continuously working against our success. This force was programmed to work against our progress, to drag us down from mounting up, to blow off our lights not to shine, to hinder us from accelerating, to confine us from living our best, and to make us struggle in our quest to succeed. There is nothing anyone has done to provoke this force, but the force is working against us. Whether you believe there is a force against us or not; the fact remains; there is a force working against your success.

Different beliefs in the world reckons there is a force against humanity, but due to various doctrines, that force is recognized differently. Some believe that force is the devil, and some think it's just life issues. Some think it's only the hearts of mean people, and some believe its witchcraft and so forth. While we may argue on who's that force, we all agree that there's a fight we're fighting.

Whether you're a Christian, Muslim, Buddha, Ancestral, or even Atheist, we'll experience the blows from this force in the same way. Also, if you don't believe there is any force working against our success, I give you few paragraphs from here, and you'll nod your head in agreement with the battles we're all facing.

Law of gravity

"Gravity may put the planets into motion. but without the divine Power. it could never put them into such a circulating motion as they have about the Sun. and therefore. for this as well as other reasons. I am compelled to ascribe the frame of this System to an intelligent Agent.

— Isaac Newton

Let's first look at the concept and content of gravity, which will give us a clear relative picture of this force.

Gravity is known to be the force always withdrawing one direction; downwards. A scientist named Isaac Newton discovered this force. When an apple fell from its tree, it triggered his mind. Being curious about it, he arranged more experiments and tests until he came up with this theory of a downward force, always pulling down every object that stands above the ground. This discovering made sense while still didn't make sense. It made sense concerning some objects while it didn't make sense to other objects.

While a thrown up stone will eventually return because of this downwards force, a bird can fly without being pulled down. A bird comes down because it chooses to come, not because it's being pulled down. It means gravity works on particular objects. This leads to a discovery journey of another law, the law of arrow dynamics.

Every time you go up

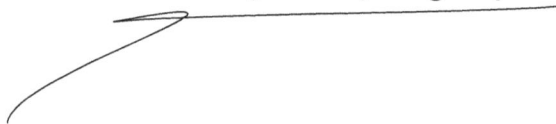

The same thing happens in our lives. Each time we try to advance, a force pulls us back. While this gravity can be interpreted differently, its characteristics are common across all different beliefs and tribes in the world. We can all commonly relate to the effects.

Every experience trying to put you down, obstruct your progress, and kill your energy is coming from this force. It uses negative thoughts and people to discourage you. It uses rejections to stop you from progressing. It uses failure and loses to destroy your passion. It uses disappointments to terminate your efforts, and it also uses fear to bolt you back. While our beliefs might differ in interpreting the source of our problems, we can all agree that these situations are the reason success isn't easy. They're the reason we always have to sweat to achieve.

We can all concur that with deficiency of fear, failure, loss, disappointments, negativity, and rejections, we would all attain our dreams with ease. Some of you are where you're because fear is pressing you back, fear of losing, of being judged, of not being good enough, and fear of being rejected and hurt. Fear is delaying your life, and you're daily battling through prayer and hope that one day you'll rise victorious.

What about rejections? Rejection obstructed you from attempting, swapped your dream, and abolished your faith. That's what the force of gravity wants to accomplish in our lives, to tow us back whenever we dare to rise.

So what does it take to overcome fear, rejection, disappointment, failure, and loss? The good news is that it's not all objects that fall for gravity. Other objects actually succeed against gravity, and that's where we find hope. In life, we have people who become successful, while others remain poor. Those who are poor might think it's impossible to succeed based on their struggle with gravity. But those who are rich believe everyone can become rich, again, based on their adventure with gravity.

When a stone keeps falling back whenever it's thrown up, it will believe in the impossible to be on top. Still, when a bird keeps rising regardless of gravity, it will end up believing in the possibility of being on top. These two believes are fostered by experience against gravity.

I believe this is what made the Wright brothers to believe they can actually build a flying transportation. While Isaac said everything that tries to go up, gravity will pull it back to the ground, the Wright brothers looked at the bird that wasn't affected by that law, and started to figure out how does the bird beat gravity.

Law of Arrow dynamics

For you to overcome the force against you, like birds, you'll need to apply the law of arrow dynamics. You must know how to absorb the power meant to destroy you into a propelling force that will compel you into your dreams. It will be best if you learn the art of turning fear into faith, negativity into motivation, rejections into directions, loses into lessons, and disappointments into rearrangements. But for you to be able to apply the law of arrow dynamics, you'll first need to be equipped with the power to press on.

There are two powerful verses in the bible concerning these things. *"In all these things we are more than conquerors."* And the second one reads, *"When the enemy comes in, like the flood, the Lord will raise the standard."* We were created with durable material and absorbing features to conquer and rise far above the forces against us. But it takes the power of pressing on for us to have the ability to turn negative experiences into positive ones. When you don't have the power to press on, you won't have that ability. The power to press on is the ability to overcome gravity.

Chapter

04

THE POWER OF HUMAN BEINGS

*T*his chapter is our final brick on the foundation that we've been developing. I hope so far you've relished building up the momentum, and reading this shows that you've committed yourself to discover this power, and I believe you're the reason I carried the burden to write this book. Losers have quit, and only winners have made it this far. I wanted to tell you that you're a winner, but I know you know that very well.

In this chapter, I want to show you the power of humans, or rather the spectacles which human beings have done under the sun through the power of pressing on. If any species can never be halted, it's humans. These inventions will make you appreciate the aptitudes carried by each individual on earth. As humans, we've proved that when you tap the power of pressing on, no mountain, no river, no thought, no failure, no loss, and absolutely no force of gravity can stop you from turning your wildest dreams into substance.

Begin to look around and contemplate the inventions of humans. The things that humans have created and built under the sun, incredible. It's humans that made spaceship transportations. It's humans that manufactured airplanes that fly in the middle of the sky. It's humans that created submarines that crawl in the bellies of oceans, and it's humans that build small devices that connect people far distanced apart. If I can begin to describe every great invention a human being has created, I'll not stop.

I'll show you exactly where we get this creative power, and why I think the human invention of robotics is one of the most powerful, and the long-time anticipated design of them all. I am about to dive into my spiritual elements right now and it's going to be enlightening. Fourth industrial revolution here we come! Ready?

Our Source of Creativity

I'm the guy who finds it weird to believe in things that create themselves, but weird enough to believe in the uncreated creator. Imagine the iPhone created by a big bang? Even Bitcoin disciples believe there's someone behind the existence of the cryptocurrency.

I believe that the creativity of humans is sourced from the creator of humans. A child is very likely to manifest the talents and personalities of his father because everything reproduces after its kind. Therefore away from the big bang theory, and I'm not about to start a debate here, but merely stating facts. I believe Elohim created the creation. That's just a superior name to use, otherwise well known as God.

The link between human creation and God's creation is so perfectly replicated that disputing the relationship between humans and God; it shows an unwillingness to relearn and accept the facts. Human beings have imitated God's creative ability so well, and the best part about it is that God told them to do so.

In the book of Genesis, we read about the creation that journeyed six days, which sounds so magical yet so real. After God creates all these things, on the sixth day, he decides to reproduce himself. He creates a man in his image and likeness and then commands them with blessings to be fruitful, multiply, subdue, replenish, and dominate. Isn't it precisely what we're doing?

Like God

I want to highlight something compelling here, and by the way, before I do, let me freshen some air first: God's image doesn't have color. God is the Spirit, and spirits don't have color. I don't know where you get that black picture you call the devil, and the white (although white is this page) drawing you call Jesus/God on your wall. When we talk about the image of God, we talk about the shape, features, and abilities. God has two ears, two eyes, one nose, one mouth, two hands, two legs, and he can see, smell, talk, and feel like us. Now that the air is fresh and no book will be burned, let's continue.

When God made us in his image and likeness, it was like a father who gave birth to a kid that resemblance the image, qualities, and personalities of his father. Beyond just carrying the image of God, we can also do what he does. We can create incredible things like him, make impossible things possible as he did, and perform astounding stuff as he does. But before God reproduced himself, he first produced things that didn't resemble his image nor personalities. He created animals, trees, earth, galaxies, and all these lights, but none of them carry the full qualities and abilities of God.

Humans began to substantiate and exhibit the same creative ability inherited from their Creator. Think about this: Are you aware that a lot of things humans have created were imitated from nature and animals? Ponder on that for a moment.

Thomas Edison just looked at the star lights and resolved to create a bulb. Henry Ford looked at the tiny insert called "Bentley" and aped it's shaping to develop a vehicle. The Wright brothers looked at eagles soaring above the clouds and decided to create an airplane. Richard Trevithick shaped his train invention after the millipedes. Cornelis Drebbel designed submarine after the likeness of whales. And so many other products created after the shape of nature. Even fashion designers copy animal appearances such as snails and peacocks.

But even after humans have created these great inventions, they weren't at the peak of their creativity yet. After God created nature and animals that didn't resemble himself, he reproduced after his image and likeness. Following the footsteps of our Creator, after all these inventions which none resembled ourselves, we finally reproduced after our image and likeness, we made robotic humans. A human-machine that can talk, sense, and do the things we can do, while looking exactly like us.

After our own Image & Likeness

Welcome to the fourth industrial revolution, where humans finally created robots after their image and likeness. I pray that like we turned against God, they don't turn against us. At least God was smart enough to distance himself far away from that possibility. Unfortunately, we share the same occupancy with them. So good luck, humans, may your kids never turn against you, Amen!

These human inventions didn't come easy, but when an idea is connected to the power of pressing on, it's bound to happen no matter the odds. If Wright brothers came to you and said, "We're creating a big machinery bird that can transport people across the globe, flying above the clouds." That would sound crazy. Henry Ford says, *"If I asked customers what they wanted, they would have said a faster horse."* Why? Because they never imagined any other better transport than horses. But the man conceived it, and without having any reference to the existence and possibility of what he saw, he believed it could come to reality — the same trait of God in creation.

If I told you ten years ago that we'll have machinery humans who will work like us, sense like us, function like us, and even talk like us, you could've thrown me out of the window. The old movie, **the gods must be crazy**. Remember it? An empty bottle of coke falls on the land of Khoi people from the sky. Not knowing what it is, they wonder why God would send them something like that. The bottle looks strange to them until they give it a purpose in their family. A lot of things always look crazy until they become familiar — the same thing with ideas. When you conceptualize a never-seen-before idea, people might deride and laugh at it. Please don't blame them. Make it a reality, and they'll soon embrace it.

More than a Miracle

For every invention of humans, it didn't only demand creativity to accomplish. Unfortunately, when God deployed us here on earth, he forgot to conceal in us the power to speak a miraculous airplane into existence. Instead, he only gave us the ability to press on.

How many failures do you think it took Ford on his first car? How about Wright brothers? As for Thomas Edison, it took him **1001** times to get the bulb right. How can such a small thing priced below R500 take someone that long? Was it because Thomas was just not blessed with intelligence? Well, not exactly, it took the pressing on to get it right eventually. If he had no power to press on, he could've given up at 3rd attempt. That's precisely where most people throw in the towel. Maybe it's because Jesus rose on the 3rd day, I don't know. But people without the power of pressing on, give up early. The worse part we give up trying to achieve something that someone, somewhere, has already proven that it's achievable.

But imagine this man, refusing to give up on something that he has never seen before? What if what was needed to burn the light could only be found in galaxies? Honestly, if that were me, that theory could've been my conclusion on the 5th attempt. But when the power of pressing on it's working behind the idea, you won't stop at anything until you make it work.

Even in this fourth industrial revolution, humans continue to demonstrate their creative ability, combined with intellectual power, critical thinking, and the power to press on; we're still to witness more magnificent wonders on earth. Someone said there'll soon be a machine that can bath, cloth, and feed you. When it comes to what human beings can do, all things are possible.

Through the power to press on, we've seen humans constructing roads where they shouldn't be executing them. The longest sea-crossing bridge in China spans 55km (34 miles) and connects Hong Kong to Macau and the mainland Chinese city of Zhuhai. I mean, think about it; how do you instill beams in the water? The worse part, not just any water but the sea! If you presented that idea to me, I would've given it two days to stand. But to this day the bridge is still standing, carrying all sorts of big trucks. How about the roads in the mountains? Humans are capable of erecting the N1 highway to heaven. God better be careful, one-day humans might knock on his door. But he knew about these powerful abilities we carry at the tower of babel. God himself admitted that these people could be my next-door neighbors soon, and given the party noises they'll make every weekend, I better distract their plan. Had God not done that, right now, I would be asking sugar from my all-loving, generous neighbor, Jesus.

It's in you!

Humans have been conferred with the power to achieve anything, but unfortunately, many haven't patted into that power. You're also carrying that power right now. You were born with it. Whether you're a Christian or not, whether you believe in God or not, you were gifted with the ability to press on.

It's this power to press on that empowered Thomas Edison to try **1001** times. It's this power that helped Steve Job find his way back to Apple after being fired. It's this power that compelled Fredrick, the founder of FedEx, to risk his last cash at the casino to rescue his company from bankruptcy. It's this power that still convinced Nelson Mandela, upon his release, to continue with the same agenda that got him locked 27 years in prison. It's this power that encouraged Thomas Edison to persist in rebuilding even when the fire burned down his factory, losing over $2 million worth of assets. It's this power that propelled Branson to own airlines, trains, and spaceship cars even after dropping out of primary learning institution.

Anyone you admire, who achieved greatness, has realized that by tapping into this power. They immersed themselves and believed in this power to press on. And for you to perform like them, you must immerse yourself into this power.

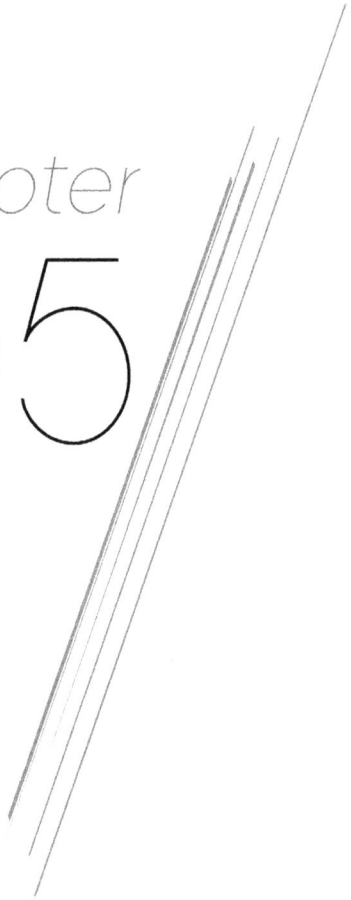

Chapter

05

THE
POWER TO
PRESS-ON

You've probably heard about this power before, but not as a power. Many people have preached it in schools, in churches, in seminars, and even on YouTube, but you've never conceived this far about it.

It is with absolute pleasure to reveal to you the power to press on, the energy that was behind Edison's **1001** attempts, Mandela's **27** years imprisonment, Job's second success at Apple, and Jack Ma's success after rejected more than the unification of your fingers and toes.

Purpose

"The purpose of life is to live a life of purpose."

— *Robert Byrne*

According to the Oxford dictionary, the purpose is:

1. "The reason for which something is done or created or for which something exists."
2. a person's sense of resolve or determination.

The purpose expressed in this book is derived from the second definition of the Oxford dictionary, with my emphasis based on experience, which is:

"the persuasive vision of transformation fused by an unquenchable sense of achieving it."

A vision of transformation in your mind, which persuades the future better than the present, giving you a strong sense in your spirit and soul that you were born solely to fulfill it, that's purpose. Now the most potent keywords here which link together it's the vision and the sense of achieving. These keywords are the most robust segments that surpass the energy of passion, intellectual power, and functional power.

Now, let's talk about these two segments and see why, when fused, makes purpose such a powerful force.

Vision

"It is a terrible thing to see and have no vision."

— *Helen Keller*

Y ou can also call it a dream or just an idea, but the vision is when your mind apprehends the distinct possibility of the future, which insinuates better outcomes than the present.

"If you can see it, you can achieve it." Right? Well, it depends. Vision alone cannot be enough to help you achieve. Vision gives direction. It illustrates a way to pursue. I guess that's where our recited quote comes into play, that if you can visualize where you want to go, you'll find a way to get there.

If you want to visit a particular town you've never been to, all you need is to see its buildings even from distant, then you can figure out the way to get there. But imagine trying to journey to a place you're clueless about its locality direction. Yes, I know about navigators; but here we're not talking about devices that superseded natural skills. Before navigators, we used maps to identify the direction, and then embark on uncovering away there. You won't use the navigator to get to your dream, but an imagination to map the route.

Life wasters

Vision gives us direction and focus. That's why every company has a vision, and the bible says, *"Where there is no vision, the people perish."* Which means people perish because they don't know where they're going.

The Hebrew word *"perish"* used there it's fascinating. It doesn't imply people begin to reek as food does. But rather *"waste."* People without vision waste their lives. That's what the scripture says. And that's true because if you can embark on a place without the knowledge of its direction, you'll waste time wondering around. That's why the direction is fundamental in life. If you don't have it, then you're wasting your life. Life is not just breathing, eating, sleeping, and repeating the circle. Life is more than that.

To further show that life is more than breathing, the story of Jesus' ministry provides an interesting perspective on what life is. Jesus tended to tell people who were healthily breathing that if they accept him into their lives as Lord and Savior, they will have life, and those who reject him don't have life. Now think about this: he was talking to people who were alive, not to the corpses. But yet he implied that they don't have life. How? Then life is more than just breathing.

Life is *"purpose."* What does your existence mean to yourself, your family, and even to the world? Does it mean you're assigned to accomplish a dream that will positively reshape your family and the world? The reason a lot of people are *"life wasters"* is that whatever goal they're trying to achieve is driven by selfish ambitions. They want to gain for themselves, not for others. When you find life, which is the reason you were born, you'll realize that it's more about others than it is about yourself. It's about impacting the lives of others, which in turn fulfills you. But when you don't live purposefully, you are wasting your life.

Typical Israelites

There is a story of Israelites spending 40 years on a journey that was supposed to take them a week. Not because they were not skilled enough to reach the destination faster, not because their God had forsaken them, not because they lacked the intelligence to navigate to the promised land, but because they failed to connect strongly with the vision of the promised land. Their minds were filled with the past and their current conditions. They complained about where they're and prefer to have been left in Egypt. Out of the twelve spies that went to the place, only two could believe in the dream while the ten still couldn't adopt the vision into their minds. The ten didn't make it because they could not see the possibility, which resulted in them lacking the power to press on, and the two later arose to lead the rest into that vision because they embraced the potential of the dream.

Vision is an essential element in your purpose because it sets you in motion. You know why you're alive, what exactly you must accomplish, and you can measure your life's value based on it.

Sense of Achieving

"Your daily behavior reveals your deepest beliefs."

— *Robin Sharma*

***

V ision alone doesn't become effective until you connect it with the sense of achieving — a bond between your heart desire and your idea. Sense of achieving empowers your vision, which builds up the compelling drive to accomplish the vision. Alone, vision cannot be a purpose, and a sense of achieving cannot exist without it. The predicament comes when you carry a dream that isn't illuminated by a sense of achievement.

Vision it's the bulb, the sense of achieving is the electricity, and the light in the room is purpose.

When vision is absent, the sense of achieving has no intention to supply with power. When a sense of achieving is missing, the vision has no ability to come alive, but when the two connects, a purpose appears in the room.

Too many people carry visions without obsession. Obsession is more subconscious than it is conscious. It's not like you tell yourself to obsess with it, but you find yourself divulging, researching, and striving to make it work.

Don't you think it took obsession for Edison to keep going even after failing so many times? When asked why he kept trying after failing so many times, he gives a response that the journalist doesn't expect. *"I've never failed, I just found 1001 ways that didn't work."*

When you're obsessed with what you see, it becomes a purpose for your life. People with purpose live with an emergency for achievement. They feel the urgency to achieve their dream.

I am going to share with you five traits of people with purpose, but before I do, I want to show you once more why Steve Job and Thomas Edison kept going even when conditions wrote them off.

Steve Job's Secret Power

As an Apple founder and pioneer, Steve Job had an absolute privilege of power, which others didn't have. When he was fired from Apple, which he built from scratch, he got fired with the power that established the company. When Steve was walking out of those buildings, leaving his position behind, the benefits and roles, he walked out with something more potent than the CEO position and millions of salaries.

When Thomas Edison witnessed his factory burning down with a damage of $2 million worth of assets, he was standing there, watching the ashes, still carrying what made him build the factory. These men lost the results but still had the roots. They lost the effects but still had the causes within themselves.

When the board of Apple dismissed Steve, they didn't say to him, *"By the way, leave your mind behind as you walk out of that door."* When Thomas's factory burnt down, his mind was not in the fire. That was the most potent secrets which later bounced them back, higher than ever before. But why their minds? Because the brain is the system that carries the vision which is needed to produce purpose. If the system crashes, then there won't be a prompt to breed obsession.

From Valleys to Cyber

These days we see fewer countries fighting with troops of soldiers because as we migrate to digitalization, wars also migrate there. The next national wars will be executed online. Cyberwars will be as real as physical wars. NSA Data Center Experience 300 Million Hacking Attempts Per Day. And it's also reported that hackers attack every 39 seconds. We have recently witnessed the conflict between US president, Donald Trump, and the Chinese mobile giants' company, Huawei, due to Trump's accusations that Huawei's devices are spying on Americans. Why would Trump react like that towards just a harmless-looking device?

He understands the migration of war from physical to digital. Today, every nation will have to invest millions into cybersecurity than it does on physical defense force. The first place to conquer war will be on cyber, not in the valley. Even terrorists are working hard to develop hacking skills that can empower them to get into national security systems, steal the information of their plans, use their data to destroy them.

It's a systematic fight we're on. It means cybersecurity is a priority on the defense list. Although this is new in terms of administrative systems, yet to human life, that has always been the case. Our minds are the systems that administrate our lives, but yet we have the weakest security systems deployed to protect this system. If the terrorists can attack a country and manage to destroy its buildings, steal its money, and kill the people, but not touch its systems, then that country will rise again. But if the system can leak, that country will be captured. Systems preserve everything.

Mental System

The reason why Steve and Thomas were able to rise again was that they still had their systems with them. The very same system that helped them start and succeed at first was still in place to help them begin and thrive again. How your life is growing reflects the systematics operating in your mind. As long as you have functional brains, you can rebuild yourself and regain your life.

The mental system is critical to functionality. It must be kept stronger and protected at all times for you to stay active and productive. Every power is created in systems, and they're responsible for control. If you want to be the most powerful person on earth, develop the most powerful system. And a system is a set of two or more things working together to achieve a specific goal.

The happenings in your body, career, business, family, or health, are results of these two: a result of your mental system performance or a reason for your mental system performance. Let me explain; fear attacks your mind because (*a reason*) it wants to weaken the performance of your psychological system. On the other side, living in fear is the result of possessing a weak mental performance. So fear can be both a root and a result of your mental performance. Nelson Mandela says, *"The brave man is not the one who does not feel afraid, but he who conquers that fear."* Fear will attack you to exhaust your mental system, and your defeat or victory over those attacks will report about the state of your psychological system.

Losing a job or a business, being broke, and in debts, being unhealthy and sick, is related to your mental system, either as a result or reason. So you must develop the most vigorous mental defense around your thoughts and ideas, to stay more stringent when life becomes hard.

If you're always sick, broke, in debts, and losing relationships, it will help to diagnose your mental system and see where you've weakened it.

You might ask, *"How do I diagnose my mental system?"* There are five traits of people of purpose that reflect an excellent performing mental system. Your mental performance reveals the power of intention you have in your life. Weak performance means you need to be more intentional, and firm performance means you're most intentional. It's worth highlighting that a robust system doesn't mean you won't be attacked, and doesn't mean you'll always feel energetic, but rather at the end of the day; you'll always find a way to predominate against the moment.

Chapter
06

FIVE TRAITS OF PEOPLE WITH PURPOSE

*T*he purpose of these traits is to distinguish between those who couldn't conquer and those who've emerged. Some people might have one or two of these traits, that doesn't mean they are purposeful. Intentional people possess all these traits, not just some of them.

We talked about positional power for physical change, intellectual power for financial, academic, and entrepreneurial development, at the necessity of three segments, knowledge, wisdom, and understanding. We also talked about mental systems. Now, as we'll go through these traits, as you'll be diagnosing yourself. Check which qualities you have and which ones you need, and then later, you'll find practical steps on how to get yourself in the same company of great achievers. But for now, let's dive into these five traits. So Butler-up!

#1   They're Positive

"It's most important that you surround yourself with positivity always. and have it in your mind at all times."

— Tyler Perry

It's one thing to be positive on a sunny day, but to maintain that positivity in the storm, now that's a real deal. If you want to tell if someone is positive or not, don't consider them in their excitement. Everyone is positive when they're excited. But real positive trait is seen when you just got fired from work and when the lights are off for weeks. When there is no food on the table and when the doctor diagnoses you with a chronic disease. When your business closes down and when you lose all your investments. That's when we know whether you're a positive person or not.

Unfavorable conditions in life provide us with an opportunity to see whether we're positive.

Story of Watson (IBM)

One of the young executives at IBM Company made some wrong decisions that cost the company several million. When he was summoned to the office of the CEO, Thomas Watson, the young man was ready to accept the consequences. But before he would let Watson fire him, he felt a need to express how sorry he is about the financial loss he caused. While the young man gave what he thought to be his last speech; Watson's reply shocked him, but most intriguing; the response revealed why Watson managed to grow IBM into a giant company. He said, *"Young man; we've just spent a couple of million dollars educating you."* Even when millions were gone, Watson remained positive, for he saw the mistake as a lesson learned, not as a loss occurred.

You can only handle a bad situation this way when you're intentional about success because the purpose you're pursuing is more significant than any loss. Everything has to work towards fulfilling that vision, even adverse outcomes.

Thomas & Steve

In 1914 Thomas Edison's factory in West Orange, New Jersey, was virtually destroyed by fire. The damage was recorded to have exceeded $2 million, and all Thomas' life work went up to smoke and flames that December night. The next morning, Edison looked at the ruins and said, *"There is great value in disaster. All our mistakes are burned up. Thank God we can start anew."*

In his speech to graduates at Harvest University, Steve Jobs shares with them about his life journey. *"Being fired from Apple allowed me to start afresh, and the feeling of being a beginner again was amazing."* This is what he had to say about being fired from the company he built from nothing.

In such oppressive circumstances, the attitude of these people remained strongly unbelievable. Didn't they feel pain? Of course, they are humans. There were some bleedings and tears, but with intentional people, the next step is always more crucial than the previous one. But why would some people have the strength to remain positive in dark times while others shutter in pieces? Well, remember the mental system we discussed? This is where it becomes most significant. These individuals had all the proper segments in their mental systems to prevail. The vision and obsession about who they wanted to be in life allowed them to build strong systems of success in their minds that will ensure their lives keep accelerating even in times of brokenness.

It takes Purpose

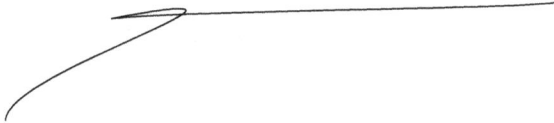

When problems weight you down, your purpose will press you up again. A positive attitude is a result of purposeful living. If you conduct a close study on your friends and family, you'll notice that all the negative folks don't have a sense of achieving and clear goals of who they want to be in life. There's nothing about the future they're obsessed about or working to accomplish. But if you check the positive folks, you'll realize that they're focused on fulfilling some visions.

It takes purpose to stay positive, to keep persevering even when everyone leaves, and to keep expecting amid draught. All great companies were built with a positive attitude because they were purposeful in their inventions.

People of purpose also remain positive because they always see opportunities in unfavorable circumstances. They don't focus on what's happening, but rather what advantage can come out of all that. The young executive saw a loss of millions that will financially slow down the company, but Watson saw the young man who just become the million-dollar asset for the company, with the lessons he learned from the loss. He can now gear up the company with great enthusiasm to recover the damages. Headlines and Journalists saw a tragedy, a man losing control of the company he laboriously built from nothing. But the same man saw an opportunity to create a new exciting venture that will add to the portfolio of his great achievements. Had Steve not been fired from Apple, he would've never started NEXT and would've never met his wife. Life connects the dots elegantly when you persist positively.

#2	**They Plan**

"A goal without a plan is just a wish."

— *Antoine de Saint*

~~~~~~

*U*ntil you plan, you'll never progress. How do we know you're progressing when you don't have any plans to follow? If I may ask, do you have a plan? I mean a plan, not a wish? Have you documented it? Because until it is recorded, it remains a wish. What is your plan?

Many people hate to be asked that question because they don't want to face the reflections of their wishful thinking. There's a famous saying, *"if you fail to plan, you plan to fail."* Maybe you're struggling with making a plan because you don't know where to start or how to go about it. Despite many articles and books you've read about 'how to plan,' you still find yourself struggling. I believe nobody can teach you better on how to plan than purpose.

Honestly, if you've been following everything I've been saying in this book, you'll understand why it's hard to try plan when you don't know your purpose because your purpose is your plan, simple.

If I see myself speaking to millions of people across the globe, that's enough to get me started with planning. How do I get there? Do the research and read more books about what you want to achieve. Find people in the same industry who've already achieved what you're trying to accomplish. Read biographies, and then all that information will guide your next steps. Do you see where it all begins? With purpose!

When you don't see yourself in the future, when you don't feel any strong feeling of being alive, you'll hardly manage to have a solid plan that can stand the test of time. Purpose drives planning.

Not a Goose

One of the benefits of purpose is focus. If you don't have a proper plan documented according to your vision, you'll be hurled into a lot of distractions that are time-wasters. Jim Rohn went from pennies in the pocket to be a millionaire in five years. He links everything to planning; that before he met his mentor, he was earning pennies with no plan of who he wanted to become in life. At the age of 25, he had a family, with creditors looking for what belongs to them. He speaks about how his mentor transformed all that by first engaging him into a written plan. Once Jim got the planning right, the next five years, he went on to become a millionaire. In his seminars, he humorous says, *"I discovered I was not a goose."*

But I'll tell you why many of us are hesitant to plan. We're ducking disappointments. When you plan to obtain a degree in three years, then you slack behind in other modules, stretching your period to four or five years, you feel like a derelict looking at your plan. To avoid that feeling, you instead roll with the flow. You preferably don't want to see failure as failure but as just unfairness of life. Yes, I know that many people who hate planning loves singing this hip hop anthem, *"life is unfair, oh yeah, it's unfair."*

Phobia of Planning

The phobia of planning is a result of not planning within your purpose. Your plans are far from your purpose, and because they're apart, they lack obsession. People of purpose don't plan with *maybes*. Sit down with people of purpose, listen to their plans, and the things they passionately want to achieve, and you'll notice that their board is exclusive of *maybes*. They plan as if they're **100%** certain it will work out. They don't leave room for ambiguities, and you know why? Check trait **#1**.

I'm not implying that planning guarantees success. That's not what I am trying to serve across the table. But I'm bringing home the fact that people with purpose, they plan! A plan is a strategy, and like any other strategy, it can fail. But because these people are glued to the habit of planning, when plan A fails, they develop another plan still within parameters of initial intention. You've probably heard this advice, *"You need to have plan B, in case plan A doesn't work out."* Can I deal with this ideology of plan B in a moment? Please don't hold me back.

Misconception of plan B

" My love, there is no plan B."

— Melody Carstairs

*I*t's so easy for people to misdefine things, and sadly when these definitions are constructed, they become a culture spread from generation to another. When people talk about Plan B, they usually don't refer to a strategy, but a goal. There is a difference between a plan and a goal. A goal is an outcome, and a plan is a strategy you need to achieve that outcome. Let me try it with another angle; a goal is a destination, and a plan is a roadmap that intents to get you there. Now, the mistake is when people advise you about the need for Plan B, referring to "Goal B.

I'll give you a few familiar scenarios. When you apply at university to study a particular course, on your application form, they always ask you to list options B and C, in case you fail to meet the requirements of the first course. So the applicant will apply for communication science as his main desired course, then for option B, write; Human resource, and Law as option C. Now, looking at the relationship between these courses, you can't surely tell me that these are plans. Because if they were plans, then the other options would still lead him to his desired career. The question is, *"if option A was for my purpose, but I find myself pursuing option C; how am I still pursuing my goal?"*

Here's another famous scenario. Whenever you tell people that you're going into business, they always advise you to have plan B, in case the company doesn't work out. And they're not referring to your business strategies, but a degree in another field. In my case, when I dropped out of Mechanical Engineering to pursue my first business in media, I was told of how foolish I was because I should've finished the engineering so I can have plan B, aka, *"backup plan."* Can I say this: this is all crap! If my passion is in media, how is engineering my plan B? It's goal B.

A plan B must still be about the goal you're pursuing. A guy goes back to working as an administrator in a manufacturing company after failing in his business of selling clothes. And he's praised that at least he had plan B. No, he had goal B. He wasn't serious about the business.

Suppose someone is held hostage in a scary old building, and I am deployed by the national police agency to rescue him. My plan A will be to access the building from the gate. If I find resistance there, my plan B will be to break the fence. If I find strong resistance there, my plan C will be to jump over the wall. If I find the wall obstinate, my plan D will be to negotiate with the keeper. If that doesn't work out, my plan E will be to blast the entrance, kill everyone resisting me until I rescue the person. Notice that I haven't drifted away from my goal. I didn't go elsewhere to find a dog to rescue because the resistance to this side was fierce. It also took the pressing-on attitude to achieve the mission, which is what precisely people of purpose do. So when I say people of purpose press on, I mean they keep on deploying various plans behind achieving their singular desired goal.

#3 They Prepare

"Give me six hours to chop down a tree and I will spend the first four sharpening the axe."

— Abraham Lincoln

There are two places of preparation; on-stage and off-stage. If you don't prepare off-stage, on-stage will be waiting for you. Many people think they can bypass training and get away with it. One thing about skill is that you can deceive your mind into assuming you're ready, that you can give the best performance even if you didn't prepare, but you can't trick your skill. If your talent is not ready, it's not ready; whether you jump high, smoke weed, drink red bull, or roar louder than a trumpet, if your skill is not prepared, it's not ready.

Whenever you watch talent competitions, especially the most popular singing competitions, you'll get to see 90% of the participants delivering a preparation on stage. The stunts they pull there are what we deal with in rehearsals. After watching few videos of Lira or Brenda Fassie singing, a young lady convince herself that she'll go on stage, open her mouth and release that magical voice, and everyone will hold their breaths in awe of this next big star they've been searching for. When they get on that stage, they're shaking, nervous, and as soon as they open their mouths to sing, the entire room hears the voice of someone screaming for help. When she realizes that she's out of tune, trying to adjust her voice to the right tune, like a broken record, she becomes a mood killer. She thinks she's performing, and even people say her performance was severe, but I say, *"Guys, let's not be too harsh here, that was not too bad for her first rehearsal. With more rehearsals she will get it right. She'll just have to get off that stage and do it off-stage."*

The stunts often clowned on stage are what we work on to improve during rehearsals. We fix those voices, nervousness, shakings, memory gemming, and mental breakdowns. We work on refining the skill so good that by the time we hit the stage, we've mastered techniques on how to control and adjust our skills to deliver the best for the world to embrace. But because we undermine preparation or feel lazy to commit to it, we end up giving a live preparation on-stage. Pressing on is about urging yourself during rehearsals to get the skill ready for the showtime.

Value of Preparation

If you're not purposeful about your talent, you're most likely to undervalue preparation. Without purpose, people don't deliberately pursue their dreams, they don't select opportunities with clear intentions, and they don't live a purpose-driven life. They leave everything to chance. And where the purpose is inactive, the ability to press on goes in suspense mode.

It isn't astounding that in sports, most teams prepare five days a week for just one game on the weekend? Soldiers train every day, for the whole year, for years, just for in case war arises. Their purpose is to defend the nation, and they understand that they'll not be able to achieve that purpose if hard work is not invested in preparations. Every day, they press on to be ready, because they are on purpose.

It took Jesus 30 years of off-stage preparation, just for an opportunity of being on stage for three years. And in those three years, he achieved something more prominent, impacting the entire world even to this day. What about David? He was chosen as the next king at the age of 15, but he had to go for another 15 years of preparation before he could occupy his position as a king. And during his career as a king, he never lost a battle.

I was being prepared

None of the noble people you wish to be like, just woke up one day, tried their thing, and then watched the magic transpire before their eyes. I also wish life offered such a quick response, but it doesn't. I wrote many books in life, which were never finished. When I started blogging on Wordpress, I cleared my articles more than five times, because the content always sounded antiquated, and my previous writing style resembled inadequacy.

I've spoken in front of people more than I can count, in youth meetings, in the bathroom, and the lounge. I've delivered countless keynotes to the couches and mirrors in the toilets. I started writing and speaking eight years ago. I wrote poems, drama scripts, articles, incomplete manuscripts, and even songs. Yes, songs! I used to write songs and give them to one of my sisters, Thembisile, to sing. And guess what: all of those things were done off-stage and 90% of them remained off-stage. I've realized that not every book I wrote was for people, but for me. To learn formatting, styles, the tone, and how to flow with the content. It was for the sake of harnessing my writing skills and preparing my mind to master the art of writing. Even those keynotes that

I've solely done were equipping me for the day I get an opportunity to speak publicly.

Today I glance back at every platform I had the privilege to speak on, the radio stations, events, seminars, and media appearances, And I realize the impact I've imparted is beyond the years I've lived thus far.

The purpose is compelling because, most times, even the things we might find ourselves going through are preparations for our goals. There was a time in my life where I thought I'll be the next South African, Tyler Perry. For real, that's what I imagined, and even those around me agreed. I used to write dramas, and we would perform them at church. People loved them and demanded more.

Even today, I'm careful not to suggest the word "drama" lest they demand another one. I still write scripts, but not for stage plays or movies, but adverts in my media company. *"All things work together for good, for those who love God, and are called according to his purpose."* Romans 8:28, a beautiful assurance that when you live a life of purpose, things always work together for you.

So, people of purpose get prepared. Notice the variation in that statement. I'm not saying *"they prepare"* but I am saying *"they get prepared."* They prepare, means they decide to prepare, but *"they get prepared"* actually means that, by being purposeful, they will be made prepared. They're prepared by God, life events, or by themselves. Whether they're conscious of it or not, they'll get prepared. So many times preparations don't make sense, but like Steve Job says, *"You have to trust that somehow the dots will connect along the way."*

I believe profoundly in preparation, especially off-stage training. Although I might appear as a perfectionist, my overall rule is to spend 80% time preparing off-stage and only 20% delivering on-stage, to achieve 80% results. Here's one of my favorite quotes, *"If you don't give me profit, then give me progress."* And progress will always lead to profit, always!

Steve and his Macintosh

After dropping out of his course in college, Steve Job says he stayed for another six months in college, attending any class that interested him, even though he knew he wasn't going to be credited. He then started attending a typography class, which he enjoyed a lot. Although it looked like a waste of time attending classes you didn't register for, Steve records that those lessons became very impactful when he was building Macintosh, because it went to become the most powerful and advanced computer even in terms of typography.

Had he not dropped out if his main course, or left college immediately, then he could've not attended typography class, and Macintosh could've never featured the typography that advanced it in the market. That's why Steve states that you have to trust that the dots will connect. But before the dots connect, because some people's dots never connects. You'll have to live purposefully. Purpose is responsible for the right redirections happening in your life.

#4 They Pick Well

"If everyone is moving forward together,

then success takes care of itself."

— Henry Ford

Supportive women make great men, and humble men make great women. Purposeful people pick their relationships and friendships well because they understand those relationships are foundations that can either make or break them.

85% of great achievers never divorce, and 60% of them credit their wives for the success they have. When they talk about the days of their developments, their wives play the potter's roles. Even most great women who are married, credit their husbands for being supportive. One of the sweet photos I've seen circulating on social media was that of Serina William's husband carrying their child on the supporters' seats while cheering for Serina's exceptional performance. That melts the heart. He could've given the child to the nanny, but he wanted to bond as a father while being the number one fan for his wife

Divorcing the Richest Man

When we observed the divorce of **#1** richest man in the world (on the time of writing this book), Jeff Bezos; The founder of Amazon, the entire media, including myself, was curious to see how the proceedings will unfold. Will the wife tear down half of Jeff's power on Amazon? Will Jeff refuse that kind of demand and cause the proceedings to get messy in court, which is something journalists are begging for because their next Ferrari depends on it? All the eyes were on the couple.

The settlement of the divorce was not what the media had wished for. Journalists were quite not happy with the outcomes because that meant they'd have to find another saucy story to skyrocket their sales. But according to this trait of purposeful people, the results could somehow be expected.

Jeff's wife left things in his control, she didn't make any bizarre demands, which retained Jeff as the richest man in the world, but most importantly for him; still in charge of his company. Of course, she didn't leave empty-handed, she earned her stake in the company, but left the controlling powers to Jeff.

Should you find yourself faced with a divorce in your glory days, pray for the anointing upon Jeff's wife to locate your partner's heart. From how the divorce was handled, we can conclude that Jeff picked well.

Think about couples such as Bill and Melinda Gates, Barack and Michelle Obama, and TD and Serita Jakes. These are the most potent couples that have proved with the right person by your side; there's nothing you can't achieve. Your dreams won't seem to be a mountain, but rather just a small hill because you've picked well.

Purpose gives you guidance regarding the kind of person you need. You'll know the character and skills you'll need in a partner. When you're intentional about your dreams, you don't chase pretty faces and tight pants. You can't be dazzled by that. Instead, you'll look for the mindset, character, and skills. Will this person be equipped to handle my absurd thoughts, will they encourage me in my downfalls, will they support my risks, and will they be helpful in my burdens?

90% of divorces are results of men that are not goal-oriented. We know this because these divorces result from abuse, infidelity, and financial blackout. Yes, it also goes to women as well, that women who cheat do so because they're not purposeful. There's absolutely no desire or time for a person of purpose to abuse and cheat unless you confuse being purposeful with having money or a good career because many people have great jobs but don't have a purpose.

Winnie Madikizela-Mandela

Winnie Madikizela Mandela handled her divorce to the former South African president, Nelson Mandela, very well. Given the fact that the separation seemed unfair on her, having waited 27 years for his release from prison, only to see him return to marry another woman. Yes, they might be good reasons that are none of our business, which may have led to this divorce, but Winnie didn't throw tantrums around because she was a woman of good character. Nelson being a president at that time, went for someone else who understands the burden of that role. So he snatched Graca Machel, the ex-wife of the late former president of Mozambique, Samora Machel.

The man certainly knew how to pick. First, he chose a woman who had great character, and then secondly, he pursued an experienced woman in the role of being a president's wife. Okay, okay, I know this example won't win any grammies, because, eeuy! It's not inspirational at all. But I can't rub off the feeling that *"Man! Nel was very strategic for himself. He knew how to pick for his purpose."* Perhaps the entire 27 years in prison, he was busy constructing that move. Okay, let's stop having fun over this situation. It's not funny at all.

Relationships play the most significant role in our lives because they can jeopardize your performance with their conflicts. If you receive a thousand people praises on your excellent performance, but get home to a partner who'll give you a useless look and say, *"Be a man."* Simply because you can't fix the tap, all those thousand praises will drown in the drain, and her words will echo for a very long time, unless you're a never-mind person, more like a clown.

The people close to you must be constructive to your dreams. Those friends who never lay a brick of support on your dream must be removed. Otherwise, they'll remove every block you put for your future with criticism.

My Friend's Story

I have a friend who just came out of the marriage, which stagnated her life for years. Her ex used to discourage her whenever she spoke about her dreams. She grew up with a vision of being a model, and when she met this guy, he was a DJ, and she was a contestant at a beauty pageant. So she thought to herself, *"He's a DJ, and I am a Model, we can be a power couple and attend events together."* But after getting married, the guy settled for a secular job while she played a housewife. She became unhappy and further continued to drift away from her dream, and the treatment in that marriage wasn't making things easy for her. She was forced to choose between her vision and the marriage. With no good reason to sacrifice for the marriage, she sacrificed marriage for her dream. Today she's going after her dream and rising as one of the most talented in her craft.

At least she dared to restore her dream. But how many do we have today whose relationships have killed their goals? 80% of married women in the world have stopped pursuing their dreams because of marriages. They are discouraged, comprehended as nothing except a child-bearer and a nanny. They're not respected enough beyond the kitchen and the washing machine. It helps to become a woman with purpose because you'll know what kind of man you should accept into your life.

A purposeful man can marry a woman who doesn't live a purposeful life but still have a successful career and marriage, but an intentional woman will not last with a man who has no purpose. A hurtful separation will occur, or her job will crumple into mediocrity.

#5 They Take Risk

"The biggest risk is not taking any risk... In a world that's changing really quickly. the only strategy that is guaranteed to fail is not taking risks."

— Mark Zuckerberg

$\mathcal{J}$im Rohn says, *"Whether you take a risk or not, it's still a risk."* And then out of humor, he continues, *"I'll tell you how risky life is; you'll not come of it alive."* The point Jim is bringing across the table is that it's better to take intentional risk towards your reaching your goals than to take the risk of not giving your goals a shot.

We have two kids of risks in life, and we're all feasting on either of them. You're either taking risks for your dreams or risking your goals. The *"what ifs"* risk their dreams, and the *"hopefully"* take risks for their ideas.

It takes Risk

I used to wonder why people instead hold back into mediocrity than to give all for greatness until I discovered the concept of purpose. It's not fair to ask a person who's not purposeful to take a risk. It's like asking a fish to perform a whirlwind.

Look at every great achiever; they took risks. Bill Gates dropped out of college to get Microsoft going. Mark Zuckerberg did the same thing. Richard Branson dropped out of primary to pursue a magazine full time. What did he know about the magazine? But his fearlessness to risk has paved the way for him in places where the timid would never persist. When his magazine failed, he kept on moving to the next risk until he got it right.

Gambling save FedEx

The story of Frederick W. Smith, the man who first came up with an overnight-delivery company back in 1962 that he outlined in a paper while attending Yale University. Smith went on to become a successful businessman who took his wealth of $4 million along with another $90 million from investors to found his delivery company in 1971.

However, Federal Express failed to take off initially and was on the verge of bankruptcy. Smith took the company's last $5,000, flew to Vegas, and played blackjack. The gamble paid off. Smith made $24,000, which was enough to cover the cost of fuel and keep the company afloat for another week.

With a little more time, Smith raised another $11 million to keep Federal Express running. The company made its first profit in July 1975. Today, the Memphis-based company enjoys a total revenue of more than $3 billion.

Someone might say, *"Wow, such bravery."* Well, it happens to purposeful people. They're are willing to risk it all to make it work. They are ready to lose everything, to see their goal accomplished. When you strongly feel like there is no point in living if you don't make it work. When that obsession is on, you are willing to go utmost to make it work.

Another man who took a crazy risk was George Soros. The man in 1992, September the 12th, what is now known as the black market in England, he took a bet in forex against the pound and cashed out $1 million in a day. He was considered as the man who broke the bank of English.

The Price Tag

Maybe you don't have to risk millions on forex or blackjack, but you'll still have to take a risk to accomplish your dreams. Perhaps it's your comfort zone or your relationship; you'll have to risk. There is always a price you'll have to pay to attain your dreams. *"Dreaming is free, but the hustle is sold separately."* Thinking about it is free, but making it will cost you something. And if you receive support when you take the risk, lucky you, but many of you'll be rejected, forsaken, mocked, and fought for the risks that you've taken. You'll need your mental system to be tougher to handle the pressure.

Jesus says, *"If you try to save your life, you will lose it. But if you give it up for me, you will surely find it."* Another verse says, *"There is one who scatters, yet increases more, And there is one who withholds more than is right, But it leads to poverty."*

What you don't risk, you risk to lose, and what you risk, you risk to gain. Don't let fear have you quoting that the opposite way.

The courage to risk is found in purpose. The unification of vision and obsession is enough to drive you on the edge of risk. The great thing about purpose is that even when you risk and lose, you won't give up. You'll keep repeatedly going until you find your breakthrough. When the vison frequently plays in your mind every day, with the energy of obsession in your heart, giving in to risk will be slight.

A person who's terrified of risk lacks intentionality in their idea, and without being entirely intentional, you can't unlock obsession.

Package

*A*s I said before, these traits are not items that you can pick the ones you like and claim to be purpose-driven. They're a package, and all of them must be proven to exist in you. You must be positive, a planner, a preparer, a good picker, and a risk-taker. To clear some air, risking is not acting fooling or reckless. Putting your family on the line for your dream is foolish. If it's your house in which you stay alone, then you can take that risk, but if your kids or siblings are involved, you might have to explore other options. It's called proper risk management.

I hope you've done introspection on yourself, and now you know whether you're purpose-driven or not and whether you have the power to press on or not. In the following chapter, I'm outlining practical steps on developing a purpose-driven life. This book won't be one of those books which leave you hanging, with too many questions in your mind. Neither have I intended this book to merely inform and exposing your deficiencies with no intention of bridging the gap.

We're solving the issue of waking up each morning with zero amount of goal-orientation. We're tired of people who're just living without any obsession to achieve something significant in their lives. What's the most popular song sang at the funerals? "He was born in Limpopo, went to Thingwa primary, and attended his high school at Lekoko high school. He graduated with a teaching degree at the University of South Africa and went to teach at

Modiri High School until a short illness took his life. He leaves five kids behind." That's it? What a waste of life. What legacy did he leave behind? Will his kids inherit his teaching degree and career? We need more, and with the power to press on, you can leave a substantial legacy behind.

My ultimate goal is not to make sales, but to make an impact in your life. If I sell millions of copies but not receive any mail from you, testifying on how the book has helped you, then this book will be a failure. My success in this book won't be determined by the number of copies sold, but by the number of testimonies received.

The last chapter is exciting because it's the most impactful part of this book. You've been getting enlightened, informed, and inspired; now, it's time to be transformed.

Chapter
07

DEVELOPING A PURPOSE DRIVEN LIFE

The most asked question on earth, "How do I find my purpose, or how do I know my purpose?"

*F*irst of all, you'll have to identify yourself first before you can find your purpose. Many people want to jump the vital step of figuring themselves out. They want to shoot straight to discovering their purpose, and that's where confusion has been breeding. As TD Jakes says, "You have to date yourself first. Get in touch with yourself more deeply." He goes further to reveal an error we usually make of dating others before dating ourselves. We spend time trying to figure someone else, we ask questions to find out who they are, and we analyze everything about them until we know their likes, desires, goals, strengths, and weaknesses. Yet when it comes to ourselves, we can hardly tell about all those things. To know your purpose, you must first understand yourself.

It Takes Process

Nobody grows up knowing their purpose. I wish that were the case because it would spare us some drama. But it takes a process for you to say, "I know my purpose." In the quest to know your purpose, you'll go through a few, if not many, trials and errors. Remember all the things I did? Apart from those things becoming valuable to my current careers, I went through them, trying to figure out myself. I wish I had done it the TD Jakes way, but I didn't know that formula by then. So for me to finally say I know my purpose, I went through a journey of self-discovery while thinking it's a purpose discovery.

It doesn't mean that my journey of purpose discovery what everyone must embark on to discover their own. There is an easy and efficient way to know your reason for living, which doesn't have to consume your precious years.

Finding Yourself

Know thyself first. Let's begin there, shall we? There are many ways to discover yourself, and depending on your beliefs, your way might not be my way. As a Christian, I found myself by glimpsing at my Creator. Just like a product which Its Creator best knows, God knows me best. The first step to my self-discovery was receiving Jesus as my Lord and

Savior, yielded to the Holy Spirit for an intimate relationship, and devoted most of my time studying the bible and praying. These exercises draw me closer to God, which in turn revealed my ultimate purpose on earth.

Maybe you don't want to go through some spiritual journey as me, no sweat, there are other exercises you can do to figure yourself out. There are two most essential traits driving you daily. These things are responsible for how you live, behave, and perform in your life. Once you can identify these two things, you can then be assured you know yourself. These things will also serve as a direction to your purpose.

Interests

"The true secret of happiness lies in taking a genuine interest in all the details of daily life."

— William Morris

Looking back to my childhood days, I remember how I used to love to draw icons and cartoon characters whenever I was bored, and sometimes I would want to write, even though I had no idea what to write. But the interest to write and draw has always been in me. I had too many books that were full of junky drawings, stories, and poems. In my first company, Minas Media Group, I play an enormous role in Graphic Designs. So the drawings in my childhood have led me to be a graphic designer. On the other hand, there you are reading a book which I've written. So my childhood writings always suggested this future, didn't they?

So in a quest to find their purpose, I always advise people to start checking the things they're likely to find themselves doing when they feel bored. Models will mess up their wall rope fitting clothes in the mirror, posing and taking photos. Singers are likely to write songs and sing. Innovators will invade things in the house and put together some projects. The things you're likely to do when you're bored, are linked to your purpose. The problem is that these things look too easy to build something significant, especially in the society that has deemed only particular talents as necessary while ridiculing soft skills. And I can see people underestimate these things when I share; they expect something more dramatic.

Weaknesses vs Strengths

"Every weakness contains within itself a strength."

— *Shusaku Endo*

---

*I*f you ask anyone, "What are you good at?" Probabilities of them freezing are big. But alter the question around and ask, "What do you suck at?" Do you know what they're going to say, "Yoh! At everything!" It's one of those classic movies. The line never goes out of fashion.

Self-awareness of your Strengths and weaknesses scale the expertise you have about yourself. People who usually suck at everything suffer insecurities and low self-esteem. Every strong person you know didn't receive stronger material of the heart than yours, they didn't receive more braveness than you, and they don't rank higher than you before God. They've just mastered the art of maximizing their strengths and minimizing their weaknesses.

You need to know your weaknesses and your strengths. And heck, no! You don't suck at everything. You lier! You have things you're very good at, and somethings you're bad at.

You need to stop exalting your weak points and start promoting your strong points. But I've realized that the reason many people feel unhappy about their weaknesses is that they don't understand the concept of strengths and weaknesses. Why would God give you flaws and still expect you to be strong?

Role of Weaknesses

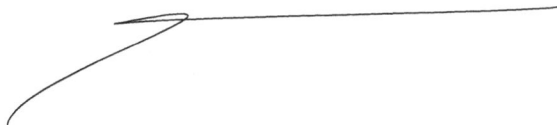

Weaknesses are meant to redirect you to your strengths. It would be best if you didn't spend time trying to develop your weaknesses, but instead focus on improving your poor habits, not your weak points. These two are not the same. Poor habits are the ones we have built over time, but weak points we're just born with them. You can't learn to be weak, you were just born with weaknesses, and that happened so you can focus on your strong points, which are necessary for your purpose. You don't need to be strong where in your weaknesses; you need to focus on being stronger in your strengths.

The other purpose of weaknesses is for relationships. If you were stronger in everything, you wouldn't need me, and relationships wouldn't be a necessity. This helps you know how to build good relationships. Imagine a band full of keyboardists only? To have an influential group, a keyboard player must suck at playing drums, and a vocalist suck at playing a keyboard. The weaknesses of these people then form a beautiful relationship. And because a keyboard player sucks at playing drums, he knows that his purpose can't be on drums, but on the keys, helping Alecia Keys deliver sweet melodies to the audience. I just had to rhyme a little right there. Didn't I? Maybe I should be a rapper. That will be the day everyone in the audience finds themselves calling for an ambulance, thinking that I am losing my tongue. Because I suck at rapping, I won't waste the little time I have on earth, trying to be the next Lecrae.

Redirection

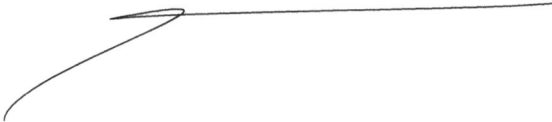

Carlos Alberto Perreira never played soccer but have successfully managed Brazil to victory at the 1994 World Cup, the 2004 Copa América, and the 2005 Confederations Cup. He was also voted the IFFHS World's Best National

Coach in 2005. He worked with the squad as a fitness trainer until he was qualified to coach them.

Most people think being passionate about sport means you're a player. There are many roles found in games, and perhaps your passion is connected to some of them. You can also be passionate about music, and find yourself managing other artists, composing, or merely producing their songs.

Once you figure out your strengths, you begin to form relationships with those who're skilled in your weaknesses. Find your interest, locate your weakness and strength in that interest, then build valuable relationships that will help you excel in your desired dream. Jason discovers that he's interested in films. But he can't act, can't write, and sucks at directing. Instead of tiring himself with acting classes, and writing classes, or looking like a clown trying to direct, Jason realizes he's very good at videography. He then enrolls for video making course and spends his life as a senior manager in video production of one of the most prominent filmmakers in the world. Seriously, our lives should be as easy as Jason's.

This process will always happen when you go through self-discovery. First you discover your interest, secondly you find your weaknesses, and then use your weaknesses to find your strengths. Finally, use your strengths to achieve your interests. At that last stage, now you're purposeful.

My Fair Share

You don't find your weaknesses to strengthen, but to gain awareness on areas you should withdraw and those you should advance. I can provide well-outlined steps on how to make your business or idea work. I am very good at that. I have a razor-sharp eye for solutions. But I've also discovered that in my efforts to materialize my ideas, I'm not quite good at the implementation stage. During the process of execution, I tend to turn functional strategies into failures. I've given people steps and systems to follow in their brands and businesses, which worked super high, and out of gratitude, they praise my smartness and wish to be me, not knowing that I have my struggles. So, out of frustration, I began to examine myself, to identify the bug and fix it.

I then learned that the reason I struggle at implementing is that I overthink a lot. I'm probably the most overthinking folk on earth. At first, this posed a weakness that I should overcome. So I tried to overcome it, only to gain more frustrations. It was until I learned that overthinking is not a weakness, but a strength that I began to be productive in it. It becomes a weakness to implementers, but for advisors, it remains the most potent strength that helps them devise solutions. Had I not been an over-thinker, I wouldn't be able to solve problems efficiently. I find solutions so fast and at ease that sometimes it puzzles me. Because some people are very good at carrying out instructions, when an over-thinker meets an energetic implementer, they form a balanced and productive relationship.

Your weakness must redirect you to focus on what you're good at so that you can maximize your strengths to achieve your interests. The day you use your weaknesses to focus on your strengths and built relationships, that will be the day you develop courage, contentment, and self-worth about your life.

- What are the things you find yourself doing when you're bored? (except sleeping & eating)
- What is your keen interest?
- What are your weaknesses?
- What are your strengths?

Create Your Future

"The most reliable way to predict the future is to create it."

— Abraham Lincoln

<hr />

$\mathcal{N}$ ow that you've realized that you're fascinated by media broadcastings, or football, or writing, or running a business or whatever it might be. You have also identified your weaknesses, which have made you aware of who you'll need in relationships and partnerships. You have identified your strengths, and confidence has leveled-up. Now comes a part where you must use all of that to create a future for yourself. God has given you interests, and the bible says, "It is God who both works within us to desire and fulfill His purpose in us." It's your turn to use those tools to build your future.

Focus on your Strengths

Begin to see yourself becoming most active in your interests through your strengths. To do this, you need to identify individuals who are in a similar field of interest, follow their work, so that you can pattern your interest after theirs. Reading their biographies will fuel your obsession. The next step will be to identify those who are stronger in your weaknesses, which you'll need to bring your future into reality. Begin to build profitable relationships, and the puzzles of your future will look more appealing and full of possibilities than ever before.

Do you now realize why people fail to have confidence in themselves? They don't embrace their strengths. Instead, they're always dwelling on their weaknesses, so they remain weak. To be weak is simple; you just have to dwell on your weaknesses. And to be strong is also simple, just begin to dwell on your strengths.

After doing self-introspection, discovering my strengths and interests, I then created an exciting future around those. I began to see myself speaking to global businesses and personal brands; giving them fresh perspective of strategies for growth and success.

Once I saw that future, and following figures already flaming in that area, I became obsessed with that idea. My self-worth began to rise, and contentment became refreshing waters in scornful sunny day. I started to focused on solving problems. Today my job is simple, listen to people's problems, and provide efficient solutions. I offer them with essential steps, and they execute.

Practical Steps

"Success has to do with deliberate practice. Practice must be focused, determined, and in an environment where there's feedback. ~ Malcolm Gladwell."

— Malcolm Gladwell

• Find Yourself

✓ Identify your Interests
✓ Identify your Weaknesses
✓ Identify your Strengths
✓ Focus on Your Strengths
✓ Channel your Strengths to Achieving your Interests
✓ Use your weaknesses to build relationships and partnerships with those stronger in your weaknesses.

• Create your Future

✓ See yourself become someone admirable in the field of your interest
✓ Follow those who've succeeded in that field
✓ Read the stories of their beginnings.
✓ Become obsessed with who you want to become
✓ Use your strengths and relationships to achieve that future.

Notes

_____

_____

_____

_____

_____

_____

These practical steps will help you become a person of purpose, and they will breed out of you the five traits of the purpose-driven. Once you reach the stage of living a life of purpose, you'll begin to see the power of pressing on working wonders in your life. Remember; what distinguishes those who give up and those who succeed; it's this power to press on.

I believe this book has been beneficial in the pursuit of your dreams. You've done some introspections, made some adjustments, and, most importantly, discovered what it truly takes to achieve all your wildest dreams.

It has been great hanging with you. I've sat on your couch, traveled with you in your car, bus and train. I've sat under the tree with you, lay on the bed beside you, hanged legs on your work desk, and flew to places with you. You've been a great company.

I'll find another excuse to hang out soon.

Stay Blessed!

Keep Pressing On

www.ingramcontent.com/pod-product-compliance
Lightning Source LLC
Chambersburg PA
CBHW061951070426
42450CB00007BA/1186